Bitter8weet
VERSES

101 Poems Of
Healing, Motivation
& Inspiration

ED BREEDVELD

Bittersweet Verses: 101 Poems of Healing, Motivation & Inspiration © Ed Breedveld 2023

The moral rights of Ed Breedveld to be identified as the author of this work have been asserted in accordance with the Copyright Act 1968.

First published in Australia 2023 by Bovercon Pty Ltd

ISBN 978-0-6457893-0-0

Any opinions expressed in this work are exclusively those of the author and are not necessarily the views held or endorsed by the Publisher.

All rights reserved. No part of this publication may be reproduced or transmitted by any means, electronic, photocopying or otherwise, without prior written permission of the author.

Disclaimer

All the information, techniques, skills and concepts contained within this publication are of the nature of general comment only and are not in any way recommended as individual advice. The intent is to offer a variety of information to provide a wider range of choices now and in the future, recognising that we all have widely diverse circumstances and viewpoints. Should any reader choose to make use of the information herein, this is their decision, and the author and publisher/s do not assume any responsibilities whatsoever under any conditions or circumstances. The author does not take responsibility for the business, financial, personal or other success, results or fulfilment upon the readers' decision to use this information. It is recommended that the reader obtain their own independent advice.

Dedicated to…

Anyone who has ever ridden the emotional rollercoaster of life and survived.

Preface

I remember learning about poetry in grade 4 and 5 in primary school. I became fascinated how a poem could translate and deliver such a powerful story in just a few verses and express such a full range of emotions that could take me into the mind of the writer. Feelings of love, sadness and despair, happiness and joy and even passing on of knowledge through words of emotional wisdom learnt from experience or witnessed in another's journey through life.

I eagerly learned of the different styles of writing poetry and expressing oneself through the power of words. I could free my romantic thoughts and express the times when I was feeling lonely or depressed. I found poetry a great escape for setting free the pent-up emotions that were building inside of me. It was cathartic to be able to write and set free the thoughts that were colliding in my head.

Yet back then I was very reluctant to share any of the emotions I jotted onto a pad or book, thinking I was abnormal and that I was the only one who ever experienced these thoughts. In those times I just hid them away, and mostly after a while they were thrown out or burned.

It wasn't until I was almost 60 years old that I started to share my works on social media and was truly surprised to hear that people not only enjoyed them but found that my poems seemed to be helpful to people who had PTSD or suffered depression. They wrote to me telling me they found solace in my poetry and found it consoling that someone seemed to understand what they were going through, this was indeed an eye opener for me and helped me understand I was as normal as the next person.

I also realized I could feel other people's pain and grief and I translated what I felt into poems which I then gave back to them to let them know that someone cared and understood how they felt, though most of my writing referred to times in my own life and I used my writing to evict the pain harboured inside of me and place it on paper.

So, if you are reading this, I hope you enjoy my writings. I hope that my poetry touches your heart and helps you understand that there are people out there that know, and understand, what you are feeling, and maybe you too can go on to seek out and help others to understand that life is truly beautiful and worthwhile.

Introduction

Welcome to my book of poems, a collection of works I have written that explores the many emotions that define the human experience. From joy and love to grief and despair, each poem in this collection reflects the complex and powerful emotions that shape our lives.

Throughout this book, I aim to capture the essence of what it means to feel deeply and to express those feelings through the beauty of language. Each poem is a journey into the heart of a particular emotion, exploring its depths and complexities and revealing the ways in which it affects us all.

As you read through this collection, I hope that you will find solace, inspiration, and understanding in the words on these pages. May they speak to your own experiences and emotions and help you to connect more deeply with the world and those in it, around you.

Take your time to read them and please, my advice is not to read more than one or two at a time. I think of them as though they are food for the mind and soul, so savor them, digest them in your mind, and take time to reflect on them to get the most out of them.

For me, poetry is more than just a medium of artistic expression; it is a way of understanding and processing the world around us. Through the power of language, we can explore the many nuances of our emotions and find meaning and purpose in even the most challenging of circumstances.

So, I invite you to join me on this journey through the emotions that define us as human beings. May these poems bring you closer to yourself, and to the world around you, as we explore together the power of emotions and their effect on our lives, enjoy.

Contents

Preface vii
Introduction ix

THE GRIEF INSIDE 1

Pain Eternal 2
Echoes of Pain 3
The Parting 4
Fulfilled And Now Empty 5
Time Looped 6
The Saddest Meeting 7
Painful Memories 8
In Constant Loving Memory 9
To Friends Lost 10
When My Mother Called 11
The Grave Recollection 12
In My Dreams You Still Live 14
The Change 15
The Job 16
The New Morning 17
Only in Dreams now 18
Heavenly Memories 19
Lost and Standing 20

    Prejudged and Wronged 21

    Sorrow, Loss and Love 22

    Unexpected Loss 24

FACING DEATH'S DOOR 27

    Footsteps 28

    Strange Peace 30

    A Loved One Passes 31

    Voices in the Dark 32

    Love from Beyond 33

    The Final Realisation 34

    The Visitor 36

    One Day 37

    For all I Love 38

    Proud to be Friends 39

    Just 'til the Morning 40

    The Calm and Beauty 41

    The Leaving 42

    The Dream 44

    The Life Traveller 45

    The Light 46

    The Lonely Parting 47

    The Mountain 48

    The Evening Campfire 50

    The Heart Plays On 51

LOVE ABOUNDS 53

    Love Eternal 54

    A Poem for my Love 55

    For All Mothers 56

    A Star of Light and Love 57

    Agape 58

    The Journeys End 59

    The Greatest Gift...60

    For My Brother...62

    Love Is Still Beautiful 63

    A Tender Moment Shared for Eternity 64

    Unrequited Love..65

    A Time Given 65

    For My Beautiful Debbie 67

    For My Brothers 68

    Love's Promise 69

    Just another Poem 70

    Merry Christmas and Love to All 71

    Ode to Women 72

    The Loving... 74

    When Souls Connect... 75

LIFE'S LESSONS 77

    For the Troubled..78

    For My Dear Friend... 79

A Poem for our War Heroes ... 80
PTSD ... 82
Heartache ... 83
The Black Dog ... 84
My True Demon ... 86
Abused ... 88
Wisdom Shunned ... 90
The Tormented Soldier ... 92
The Unknown Reality ... 94
A True Hero ... 95
Empty Words ... 96
Hidden Scars ... 97
In Dark, Lost and Lonely ... 98
The Battle ... 99
Pure Love Misunderstood ... 100
Mistakes or Lessons ... 102
Reflections of Self ... 103
My Journey ... 104

HEALING ... 107
Words of Love and Understanding ... 108
An Old Mans Wisdom ... 110
Reaching Out ... 112
My Offer ... 113
A Different Way of Thinking ... 114

A New Start..116
From True Love Born..118
Agape Love...119
Hidden Rooms..120
Catching the Wind...122
Lessons... 123
Deaf Ears Will Hear.. 124
Criticism.. 125
An Angel Sings... 126
My Gift... 128
Coloured People.. 129
Sunset on my Journey.. 130
My Paradise.. 132
Harvest of Love 133
Words of Love and Understanding 134
Conclusion..136
Acknowledgements...137
About The Author..139

THE GRIEF INSIDE

Pain Eternal

I would gladly reach out across the grave to hold
you once again,
To reach for you, take you in my arms
and wash away my pain,
Your laughter used to fill the air around me long ago,
But from this life you had your time and then you had to go
I held you in my arms and on your face did gaze,
And wondered why you left me in pain and in a daze,
Time, they say heals all wounds, but this I feel is just a myth,
The wound may heal but not the pain it has left me with,
Still, I had the gift of having you in my life
and filling it with love so full,
And for this dear son, I will always be in your debt
and forever grateful,
I loved you then, and I still love you now
my young and wonderful son,
And I will always hold you in my heart until
the day does come,
When once again we'll meet and hold each other tight,
To share the love we have, and then let our wings take flight.

Echoes of Pain

I passed you today whilst going for a walk,
I saw you standing there, though I didn't stop,
Your head hung low, and your eyes seemed hollow,
I was hoping you would not see me, or try to follow,
On a grass field you were standing there, lost in your fate,
Your shoulders hunched as if tied to a terrible weight,
Once we were so close, and we shared everything,
From the clothes on our backs, to our feelings within,
But then something happened, and we went our separate ways,
And that was the end of our happiest days,
No farewell nor goodbye, just one day you were gone,
Leaving me alone, and in pain and crying for so long,
For many years now I have mourned that fateful day,
When I received the call that you had gone away,
And still I wonder what made you do it, and why,
That you chose that day, by your own hand to die,
The pain may have ended for you my dear friend,
But for me it is now amplified until my days end.

The Parting

I look at you standing there, crying over me,
Watching your pain caused when I was set free,
I see the tears of sorrow fall down your cheek,
Tears of gut-wrenching pain that words cannot speak,
I hear indescribable sobs of sorrow coming from in you,
I want to help you, but how, I just haven't a clue,
I feel the sadness in the room where you stand,
I foolishly reach out and try to hold your hand,
I need to hold you, to touch you, and tell you it's ok,
I want to go back to change things, and stay,
I long so much to hold you close to me,
But I cannot touch you, for it is me you cannot see,
I died from complications I hear that they said,
Now my soul stands here watching,
while my body lays dead,
Suddenly I hear the call, and in front of me I see the light,
Like a torch so bright, it guides me through this night,
Whilst I long to stay and hold you again,
To help take away your crippling pain,
I whisper; "Farewell, I love you my sweet",
"I will wait for you, till again we meet",
Your head turns slightly as though you heard,
I thought you looked at me, as you spoke one word,
"Yes" you said, trying to smile through
the tears of a broken heart,
"I'll always love you" were the last words I heard as I left,
to begin my new start.

Fulfilled And Now Empty

I remember when we loved each other so,
When you told me that you'd never go,
I remember how we'd love and kiss,
When a chance to meet we'd never miss,
I remember when we'd talk for hours,
And how I would always bring you flowers,
I remember when I'd always ring,
When songs for you I'd try to sing,
I remember when I'd do anything for you,
To cheer you up when you were feeling blue,
I remember when your meals I'd cook,
And how beautiful you'd always look,
I remember when you left that day,
When the angels came and took you away,
I remember when laughter filled the air,
When I lived my life without a care,
I remember it all as now down my cheek rolls a tear,
Because in my life, you are no longer here.

Time Looped

I awoke standing on a beach shrouded in smoke,
Lost, confused, and alone, was this some kind of joke?
How did I get here I wondered, still looking around,
All around me scorched Earth and fires abound,
The flames licking the air, but I kept walking on,
In this smoking hell all sense of direction is gone,
A voice calls out, yet I know not from where,
What feeds these fires that burn everywhere,
Lost and alone, this is everything I have ever feared,
I turn to find that all my tracks have disappeared,
No way of knowing which way I have come,
No landmarks can I follow, not even a sun,
No stars, no shadows nothing to guide my way,
Just fire and smoke and a sky-coloured grey,
Just then a shadowy figure comes out toward me,
Please can you help me I shout and I plea,
I am lost and need direction, can you please help,
The stranger walks close, and in shock, I see it is me,
Walking silently past me as though he didn't see,
This happens over again as I watched in confusion,
Had I hit my head somehow and received a concussion,
It is then I understood of this place, that time seems to repeat,
That the friction of time being on hold, was creating this heat,
The more I did, the more I created to join in this group,
In this time skipped over in a constant unending loop,
I remain here still, trapped with no way out I can find,
As every moment repeats, I am slowly but surely
losing my mind.

The Saddest Meeting

I was talking to my son today when he casually stopped by,
Quietly I told him I was sorry that I never got
a chance to say goodbye,
He smiled and told me he's been travelling to worlds far away,
I pleaded if we could catch up, but an answer
did not come my way,
It was cold there while I spoke to him,
yet the sun was blazing down,
He was wearing a flowing outfit, akin to a
long white satin gown,
I told him that I missed him and wished he would come home,
That it was no longer the same without him,
now I was on my own,
He seemed to listen intently like he was hanging on every word,
How I miss my little mate so much,
whom for so long I have not heard,
You see it was his spirit that came visiting that day,
and left me in so much pain,
For he has gone over, and now all I have are
the ashes in a box where he was lain,
One day my son I will join you, and together
we will fly once more,
And above this place that we call earth on
wings of angels we will both soar.
Now back together again once more,
we will cross together into the light,
Where our love will now burn eternal and continue
to shine bright.

Painful Memories

There before me you appear once more,
A painful memory, a puss filled sore,
I start to ache, and squirm away,
Yet my gaze is locked, and here I stay,
You reach out for me, my soul to touch,
Your power over me, appears too much,
We touch, and you suddenly disappear,
While in my mind, your visions are clear,
Sliding through me, and coursing around,
My soul is yours, my heart is bound,
The colours fade, and all goes black,
Surrendered to you, I cannot go back.
The pain is gone, just like the fear,
Yet deep inside, I still shed a tear.

In Constant Loving Memory

I woke this morning and again remembered that you were gone,
And once more the feeling overcomes me of how hard it is to go on,
I still miss your company, I miss your touch, I miss your loving way,
Your calming ways in times of trouble, and the loving things that you used to say,
You gave so much love to me, and I always felt I had a home within your heart,
Always ready to forgive and move on, your wisdom and love you would freely impart,
But again, I find myself asking, how do I move on now that you are no longer here,
I think of you constantly, and I freely admit that there are times when I still shed a tear,
Believe me, I am always thankful for your time and the love you gave to me,
And deep in my heart, I keep and cling to your love and cherished memories of thee,
Thank you for the lessons you passed on and the many sacrifices that you made,
Especially for the many times you would lift me up, and your love that never strayed.

To Friends Lost

Old friend I remember how we once spent our time,
Back in the day when we where we were both in our prime,
With no constraints or barriers to keep us on track,
Flaunting the laws of the man that tried to hold us back,
I cried when you left as I would see you here no more,
Part of me died as well when you walked through deaths door,
Sometimes I thought I saw you standing there,
From the corner of my eye, you stood alone and so fair,
But when I turned to meet eyes with you again,
It always turned out to be just the same pain,
You would just fade away and again I would cry,
As memories of you came rushing in and flooding by,
I miss you, old friend but a day will come when you don't have to hide,
When together we'll mount up and take off for that ride,
Toward a sunset like brothers, it will be a beautiful sight,
When we ride off together into that welcoming light.

When My Mother Called

I heard your voice call out to me last night,
Just to let me know that you were quite alright,
Whilst I tried to find you, I couldn't see you standing there,
But I felt your love, and felt that you still care,
You called a phrase that I have not heard since I was young,
You called to me to make a joke of my bare bum,
It brought back so many memories of times we had,
And it left me feeling so incredibly sad,
I miss you mum and still love you so,
You went too soon for me to just let you go,
But now you are with Dad and Kyle and others too,
And though I am still happy, there are times when I feel blue,
I just wanted to show you so many things,
But at least you got to see Debbie and I exchange our rings,
I so wanted to make you proud of me Mum,
To show you I was successful, so you could be proud of your son,
But if you're looking down on me Mum please know I love you still,
And that till the day comes when I die, I forever will.

The Grave Recollection

I just came around again to say hello,
and ask how you are today,

I've missed you talking to me lately,
and just came around to say,

That I love you still and always will,
and apologise if I've hurt you,

Sometimes I can be so thoughtless
and without thinking, silly things I'll do,

This time I guess the hurt went too far,
and in a moment of sorrow and pain,

You changed our lives forever,
and now our friendship will never be the same,

It is you now that ignores me,
and I cannot seem to get my feelings through,

To express the real regret that I feel,
and how I wish I could make it up to you,

I want to plead and beg you to talk to me,
but I just sit here now and cry,

Holding your photo in my hands
and just keep repeating," Why?",

*My memories of past conversations remains foggy,
but I remember so much sorrow,*

*Of you feeling lost, long midnight walks,
telling me it felt like there was no tomorrow,*

*Memories of conversation so deep, telling me of
your life that brought no satisfaction,*

*Coming home one day seeing your lifeless body,
I recall looking with horrified reaction,*

*I'm so sorry my beautiful friend, for now I understand as
I sit in this house alone and cry,*

*My soul is lost, wishing I had listened and acted, but now
racked in guilt and pain, feeling I sentenced you to die.*

In My Dreams You Still Live

Last night he crept into my sleep and walked the rooms of my mind, turning on all the lights as he wandered through.

He spoke with me and left me crushed with the memories of happier times that used to be.

You hugged me once more and told me you would stay forever this time.

Yet when morning came, I faced the truth to know you were still gone, and my heart was crushed once again.

I love you son and miss you, I'm so sorry I never did more.

The Change

I watched a man's heart turn from a furnace to ice,
Scorned by too many, he paid a high price,
He once loved so freely and gave of himself,
Whoever needed help received his love and wealth,
But then they mocked him with force and sly stealth,
I watched him in pain and his writhing was so grim,
Slowly I saw the walls start to build up around him,
He started to change and gave less to those in need,
Cautious of those who used him for the purpose of greed,
I watched him harden, and then turn bitter and so cold,
This world had destroyed his heart that was once made of gold,
In the end I watched him as he sealed himself away,
Till solitary and alone, he quietly died one chilly day,
It was rumoured when the autopsy was done,
His heart was frozen inside and had died by a gun,
A bullet shattered his icy heart deep inside,
Killing him and the pain, he could no longer hide.

The Job

Have you ever tried to save the life of someone and failed,
I have, a sixteen-year-old boy, the knife that was thrust, his heart had impaled,
Then you've had to tell his parents that their son got into some strife,
That he lost his life in some stupid fight, when the other guy pulled a knife,
Faced all his friends to inform them all as well of his untimely death,
And when walking away at the end of the shift, you're struggling for breath,
Sobbing so hard as your tears that start flowing a re so freely felt,
A cruel hand this boy and his family was by life was certainly dealt,
Then after the shift you go home, and try to put it all behind you,
Tomorrow you'll put on the uniform again, and life's stupidity will start anew.

The New Morning

When the sun begins to set and the darkness rolls in,
It brings with it such sorrow, as fear and sadness begin,
All those who stand and watch,
are smitten with grief and pain,
Whilst those that enter the darkness will end their life's reign,
Yet this darkness is like night and will eventually give way,
With a new brilliant sunrise to start their brand-new day,
So, whilst we may grieve while watching this upon us beset,
For my mother comes a brand-new life and start to
follow this final sunset,
Words of love we have all spoken as
you head toward your new start,
As we tearfully farewell you on your journey,
with both love and sorrow in our heart,
Sail on sweet and loving mother whom we all love so,
and still adore,
And thank you for the memories we will hold in our hearts,
we will cherish them for evermore.

Only in Dreams Now

Dancing in the moonlight to the music of the wind,
The earth beneath our feet alive in the moment,
The air itself is electric and sparking in tune,
Clouds booming in time to the beat,
Lights flash as once again we meet,
My eyes locked on the sparkling beauty of yours,
Hands trembling as they touch your velvet skin,
Your lips touch mine and the ice on my heart melts before you,
You smile and your love fills the gaping maul in my chest,
Morning breaks and once more I stir from dreams,
Breaking light again washes your image away,
Alone I lay here saddened with heart heavy and broken,
Yet your memory dances still in my mind,
The day I lost you my world collapsed,
It is my heart that keeps your memory alive,
And your memory that alive will keep me,
Tonight, once more I will again meet you in dreams,
And once more my heart will live,
Till the day I too remain in sleeps eternal arms,
I will always love you.

Heavenly Memories

A memory fell from heavenly skies and landed in my mind,
To a time, years ago, of a happy boy that I sadly left behind,
Of his little smiling face that used to scream so loud with glee,
A boy that I would lovingly chase, as from bath time he would flee,
From the top of my head, I would tumble him, till he reached the ground,
And he would fill the room with happiness, as his joyful laughter did resound,
There were also times of worry and concern when he would be quite ill,
Times when it would feel that my world would suddenly stand still,
Then that fateful memory fell, of the day his tenure on earth did end,
The day that my heart was ripped apart, and would never heal or mend,
Many years and many tears have passed since that dreaded and awful day,
And not a day or moment goes by that I don't miss him in every way,
A small bundle of joy he was, and my love for him is still just as strong,
And though he was my son, apparently to this earth he did not belong,
But my wish is that when our time here on this earth is through,
We will all reunite together again; this I can only hope comes true.

Lost and Standing

I wait in silence locked in a dark room,
Why I am here I can only assume,
Taken from my world in the bright light of day,
Locked in darkness and now here I must stay,
What seemed so real I now know is fake,
To try to escape is a chance I won't take,
For lost am I in a world I don't know,
A world where reality is only a show,
My mind races with thoughts of what is to come,
Will I ever find my way out back in the sun,
Then lights do enter from either side of my cell,
One is sunlight and the other I cannot tell,
For it is far brighter with a magnificent white sheen,
So pure and much brighter than any light I have seen,
A voice calls out to me and asks me to decide,
A decision must be made, and from this I cannot hide,
I seem to recognise this place, I feel I've been here before,
But what to do now, I must make this decision once more,
Then my decision is made, and I choose my selection,
Feeling confident this time I've chosen the right direction.

Prejudged and Wronged

His life cut short when a car mowed him down,
He was just heading out to enjoy, a night out on the town,
Then this fool ran him over, "I didn't see him he said",
As he stares at the biker laying there, now obviously dead,
They gather and stare in morbid fashion,
But very few around, show any form of compassion,
He is just a biker, a troublemaker, life's scum no doubt,
Wearing those clothes, that vest he wears,
no doubt he's just a lout,
But off the road one stands silently, with a tear in his eye,
His heart filled with pain, he lets out a sorry sigh,
He mounts up again and rides away from this show,
His heart is heavy, and his head is hanging low,
But something is wrong, and he has lost control,
He slides to a stop, but the fall has extracted a heavy toll,
Now to a light he's been called, to enter pearly gates,
No sorrow or pain for him here, for he'll see many mates,
This place, this Nirvana, that now beckons him in,
His death so untimely, but takes it on the chin,
He thinks back to loved ones, for one last time in his mind,
To all those he loved and now must leave behind,
His only wish is that he still had the time,
To show them his love, and give them a sign,
He will travel forever now, enjoying this new ride,
And maybe one day, I will again ride by his side.

Sorrow, Loss and Love

The days are all much shorter,
especially now that you have gone,
And as the leaves fall from the trees,
I sit and listen to your song,
In the air the wind blows cold,
from the mountain air so high,
The alpine peaks are covered in snow,
that reach to touch the sky,
The sun has set, and I am left cold,
and dark, and all alone,
And I long for you to be close to me,
and come with me back home,
But you left me standing alone,
and now you are so very far away,
It hurts me so, but I know that you will
come back to me one day,
On that day I will join you,
and together in triumph we shall reunite,
And there I will stand by your side,
and fight the demons of the night,
You were the like the wind in spring,
blowing softly through my hair,
That blew so gently and so sweet,
and poured love into the air,
You gently reached out and touched my heart,
and I lowered my defences,

I can still smell your sweetest scent,
softly lingering in my senses,

Feeling your warm caress upon my face
and seeing love in your eyes.

Then came that fateful day you told me,
that you were ill and soon to die,

All I felt was my world crumble, I looked at you,
and we both began to cry,

But that was then, and much time has passed,
and I have come so far,

My wounds have healed but, in my heart,
you still live alongside that scar,

I will heal my heart completely one day,
but I will never love that way again,

The armour that I wear now, reminds me
I will never be the same,

But life goes on, and I am strong, and onward
I forced myself to stride,

With head held high and standing tall,
from the world I did not hide,

Not hate, nor ill will shall I allow to sully
your cherished memory,

For only love and kindness shall I spread,
and hope you wait for me.

Unexpected Loss

Smiles and laughter that hide from others their painful truth,
Pain concealed by closed lips, akin to hiding a rotting tooth,
Listen carefully when they speak, sometimes it gives
an unexpected view,
Of all the things that they hide deep within that
we never knew,
You see them as joyful, loving, always happy and so carefree,
Yet they look at you from behind a cage hidden within,
one that you never see,
There is so much hidden from those whom they keep around,
Always cautious never to utter a pained word or
despondent sound,
Then one day you get that awful, fateful call,
that they took their own life,
You feel the shock and horror of the loss that cuts at
your heart like a knife,
Angry, you cannot understand why and tell all that
to you all seemed well,
We could have helped him if only we knew,
or someone of their plight they did tell,
Guilt and sadness washes over you for being so blind
to his plight before,
And despite the caring words of others,
consolation can come no more,
The grief of this loss is one you feel that
you will never overcome,
But in time you will learn to live with their passing
and this feeling so blue,
And while life will never be the same without them,
for you it must start anew.

FACING DEATH'S DOOR

Footsteps

I dreamed I walked behind a dark and shadowy stranger
the other day,
Taking time to step in all his footsteps carefully along the way,
I felt and understood all his thoughts and emotions as
I walked along,
Feeling all the times he was weak, feeling
all the times he was strong,
The times he was happy, and the times he felt lost or sad,
Times when everything around him,
seemed to turn from good to bad,
Then there were the times he was high on elation and joy,
Like the time when he celebrated the birth of
his new baby boy,
But there were also moments of intense, and incredible pain,
When life seemed so cruel it nearly sent him insane,
Then his footsteps came to a sudden end
and there were no more,
For his time here had finished,
and he had walked through deaths door,
But when I turned and looked back on the steps
he had walked,
These steps that I walked in, where I felt and heard him
as though we had talked,

It became clear to me then that these steps were all my own,

*That I followed my own path, one created by
the seeds in life I had sown,*

*For this life is just a series of predetermined lessons,
and we all play the game,*

*The story for each and every one of us
plays out exactly the same,*

*And the door that lay before me was the one
that we will all walk through one day,*

*So let me take this opportunity to those that I love
and know, please allow me to say,*

*That on the day I reach that door and walk through to
greet my new start,*

*Let me tell you all I truly love you, and you will
all most certainly, live on in my heart.*

Strange Peace

Recently I found the peace I always yearned,
The freedom I believe I have earned,
To not have a single care in the world,
From all my problems I feel unfurled,
No longer from the world wanting to hide,
It feels euphoric and uplifting to be so free,
All of life's problems have now released me,
This feeling is so wonderful I want it to stay,
Looking back, I see that they buried me today.

A Loved One Passes

*Every day I care for you, and help to comfort you as
you struggle for each breath,*

*While I walk through the rooms of this house you wander
between life and death,*

*No chore is this for me, for after all these years
I still love you so,*

*And it is with heavy heart I face the truth that soon
you will have to go,*

*Thank you, my dearest love, for choosing to share
your life with me as my wife,*

*For the time we have been together have been
the best years of my life,*

*Your journey here is almost over now, but I was blessed to
share with you,*

*A life full of ups and downs, and lessons aplenty,
with a love that was so deep and true,*

*And now as you close your eyes and drift slowly off to
your eternal sleep,*

*I promise that I will always love you, and your memory in
my heart, I will always keep.*

Voices in the Dark

Welcome to the darkness and please turn off the light,
The view is so much better when you cannot use your sight,
Enjoy the quiet of the dark, and let your senses grow aware,
To all the little things you never knew lived in
the darkness there,
Let them taste and feel you, for they mean you no real harm,
They like to taste your wit, and to feed on your cunning charm,
Hear the voices off in distance, that is crying out for you,
Begging you to join them, and tell them what is new,
Tell them to be silent, for they break the quiet peace,
Tell them to be silent, and for all the noise to cease,
What brings you back again, to this your private hell,
Did you one day finally break, and from your mind you fell,
Or do come here often, to find solace in your dreams,
To join the others here in finding, what you've lost it seems,
But yours is a journey where you can mostly go back,
To walk between the worlds, upon this mystic track,
You were shown the way one day, and now you show no fear,
So now you keep returning, but why is still for me unclear,
You know the day will come when you cannot leave,
And those you leave behind will surely weep and grieve,
But for now, you are welcomed on your visit to know us all,
And return you to the living until the day you finally fall.

Love from Beyond

Come the day when the sun no longer rises for me to see,
You will find yourself waking to face the day without me,
My eyes will be locked in an endless blank empty stare,
And your company I can unfortunately no longer share,
But alas this day comes to greet us all one day,
And when it comes to meet me, I just pray,
That all of you, my family, my friends will remember with a smile,
The many times when I made you all laugh for a while,
And whilst I know that you may shed tear on the day when I leave,
And that for a while you will probably grieve,
I trust that your smile will soon return to your face,
And the void in your heart, memories of love will replace,
Invoking thoughts of happiness and laughter once more.

The Final Realisation

*So much that I wanted to do for us, but now it is too late,
The horse has bolted, and it's no use now to run
and shut the gate,
This morning we argued, and you stormed to your room
and slammed the door,
A silly argument that made no sense, and now
I sit here cold to the core,
Funny but I can't even remember for what or why
we had that fight,
Or what was so important for either of us to think that
we were right,
Only the times of love and beauty are now in
my memories eye,
And as I sit unable to move, I think back
and ask myself why,
The futility of our arguments has hit my chest suddenly,
and so clear,
As the errors of my life hit home, and down
my cheek rolls a tear,
Soon paramedics arrive and do their best,
as on the floor I lie,
I hear them working feverishly, trying to ensure that
I don't die,*

A shaded figure stands there waiting patiently for my end,
Holding out his bony hand, offering me peace,
just like a life-time friend,
My gaze falls to you standing there, wondering if I will go,
But this my dear is my final curtain,
and the end of my live show,
No second part or intermission, no encore will I play,
The futility of this life I led is why I choose not to stay,
Of all the things I thought important
I realize now, held no value,
The times that I placed money and position before love,
How I wish I understood that greed would only lead
me here to a sad and lonely end,
With a wife that no longer loved me, and death,
my only friend.

The Visitor

Dark and gloomy he stands there silently staring,
His eyes drill through me, constantly glaring,
Cloaked in dark robes, near me you stand,
I dare not reach out and take your bony hand,
The cold in your eye sockets, chill me so deep,
There is ice in your words, frosting the air as you speak,
Taunting me with threats upon which I dare not look,
Your quill at the ready to add my name to your book,
I see your offerings, all so shiny and bright,
Your only wish is to take me with you tonight,
I dare not look at you, nor the gifts you offer me,
For if I do, I will surely succumb and leave with thee,
So here I sit, alone, almost paralysed with fear,
While this cloaked figure continues to stare
and taunt me, so near,
But I just laugh and stare at him and as I fade away, I tell
him that I'm his greatest fear, and that it is
I who doesn't really exist.

One Day

One day I'll be free from the constraints of life,
Soaring through the heavens in an endless afterlife,
To visit the galaxies and planets beyond,
The stars in the sky of which I am so fond,
What life will I find what places will I see,
What wonders of life will I find that have evolved to be,
The depths of the oceans would now be in reach,
What an exciting time as laws of physics I'll breach,
I'll walk through walls, span through time,
heck I'll fly through space,
Then I'll be off to explore some other interesting place,
No cares no worries, no pain, no feeling of loss,
No work to attend and no overbearing boss,
It's not that I want to leave here just yet,
But I will leave one day, for that is a sure bet,
I'm just contemplating in my mind what it will be to entertain,
The feeling to be free from constraints, and feelings of pain.

For All I Love

When my body leaves and lives here no more,
Do not cry that I'm gone for you can be sure,
That I will be watching over you every day and every night,
To guide you through life and keep you in sight,
When you are sad or lost or feeling blue,
That is when you'll feel my arms wrap around you,
Though you won't see me please remember this much,
I will reassure you not by words, but through gentle touch,
Please feel no fear when upon your arms or face,
You feel a caress softer than any silken lace,
And when you hear the wind call your name from aloft,
It is I that will be calling to you across the distance so soft,
For when my time comes, and I can no longer stay,
Part of me will remain by your side, to guide you every day,
For my love for you is constant and will always be,
Till the day comes again when you join once more with me.

Proud To Be Friends

*One day, sometime in the future, when you find that
I am no longer here,*

*Should I cross your thoughts, or in your mind
my words you again hear,*

*I hope you think no ill will toward me, and forgive
me my faults or any tears,*

*One's that I may have made you shed, even unintentionally
over all the years,*

*May you remember me fondly and understand, that for you,
I only wanted the best,*

*And that I tried so hard to be there for you, especially
when life put you to the test,*

*For life dishes out to us all some good times,
but it also sends us some pain,*

*And all these tests that we all go through, well,
no two are ever the same,*

*But know that I always tried to be there for you,
especially in your times of great need,*

*To help you through whatever was required,
without a single thought of reward or greed,*

*I have tried to remain constant for you,
and stayed faithful and true to the very end,*

*When you read this please understand,
I am proud to have called you "my dear friend".*

Just 'til the Morning

Laying here I gently close my eyes,
as evening falls on my life,
All pain and worry have left me, as I leave this world of strife,
Your sorrow pains me to see,
and I try to hang on one more day,
But my time here has reached its end,
and you struggle what to say,
Then words just seem to come to me,
and I take you by the hand,
Uttering the words I feel and believe,
and hope you understand,
This is not farewell or goodbye my love,
only time for me to sleep,
So, till the morning I'll wait for you, my love;
please do not weep,
So let me say goodnight for now, and in the morning,
we will again be as one,
To start a new chapter of love together, that will shine as
bright and radiant as a sun.

The Calm and Beauty

He lies on the bed looking out at the light,
It swims all around him and bathes him so bright,
Figures above him flutter and fly,
He knows where he is but for that he must die,
No memory has he from where he came,
And why the light and not the flame?
The euphoria he feels brings peace and calm,
He feels the love and gentle calm,
Across the light he sees those waiting,
And hears the voices of angels singing,
No weight he feels nor worried thought,
Merely the peace he has always sought,
He starts to float towards his destination,
But stops to listen to a shadowy figure's vocalisation,
No words he hears but visions of one,
A lad who still needs him, that lad is his son,
I cannot go he says for my son still needs me,
Send me back and let me help him, is his plea,
Back he is pulled with the force of a train,
Returned to his body lying there wracked in pain,
Now a whole new chapter will begin to start,
Awake is he, yet so far from life, struggling to stay, not ready to depart,
There laying in limbo, not quite alive, yet not quite dead,
While this new journey plays out life like a movie inside of his head.

The Leaving

Have you ever heard the lonely call so faint,
Beckoning you on darkest nights so late,
When darkness creeps within and without,
Those nights you cannot scream or shout,
When thoughts so dark come creeping in,
To stir the memories you buried deep within,
You hear the voices call your name so clear,
While in your mind you're frozen in cold fear,
You turn to run but cannot, then you face him to fight,
Yet deep within, you know this is a hopeless plight,
His voice will call you again one day, and you will go,
To finally face your demons for that one last show,
Now he stands before you, and you steady your ground,
But surprisingly it's peace he offers you, on this time around,
Crumbling you weaken to him, for you are unable to go on,
Cradling you gently in his arms, he carries you along,
He whispers to you of closure and solace,
offering you peaceful sleep,
Promising to end your pain, with the peace that you seek,
Your eyes close softly as you feel yourself crossover,
A short period of darkness gives way to light,
your journey is now over,

He called you this time, and on this occasion,
you succumbed and left,

You could not stay in this life where the love you sought
is so bereft,

Life goes on for others you loved and knew,
but you are no longer here,

And the many you left now stand,
all of them shedding many a tear,

For those that knew you remember you with broken heart,

Because from their lives, they have lost such a large part,

While you are now resting in Earth's covering fleece,

And all those that loved you, pray that you have
finally found peace.

The Dream

Standing at the abyss I looked across the unknown,
To places I have dreamt of, and once or twice been shown,
It brings feelings of peace, love, sleep, and rest,
God only knows that I have done my best,
Beaten down over time but each time I would rise,
Again, to stand and fight without compromise,
But time has taken its toll now I fear,
Yet still I stand with a smile and not a tear,
I turn around to see the journey I have travelled,
And the burdens along with which I was saddled,
Good times seem to intersect with the bad,
Amongst lakes and rivers formed from when times were sad,
There were times of great joy, of love pure and great,
When these feelings alone would lift the great weight,
The weight that we carry in our lives every day,
As we learn to grin and bear it, and cope in our own unique way,
I turn back to the abyss and there before me an angel stands,
Shining bright with a beautiful smile, and outstretched hands,
I know I can go, but this is for me to choose,
And a little voice keeps asking, what have you got to lose?
The angel smiles and nods knowingly as I turn to stay,
To complete this journey and then maybe someday,
She'll be waiting once more, when I pass back this way.

The Life Traveller

He sits at the bar and looks in the mirror at the old man with the empty stare,

His eyes are tired as he looks across to the others but a smile he does not share,

Holding his drink as though it were his last valued possession, his mind in times of past is travelling,

Moments of old from times long ago he recalls them all, and his memories start unravelling,

Where did my friends go, what happened to my youth, why has everyone left me?

These and other thoughts race through his head leaving him lost, confused and unable to see,

Walking away he sees the ship waiting for him, ready to take him to his next destination,

His mind confused and his soul feels lost as he leaves so many behind, some lost in their own desperation,

"Hear me please!", he shouts and calls and begs them all to take heed and to allow their souls to glisten,

But his pleas and cries fall only on deaf ears, and he feels great remorse for those that will not listen,

Trudging now to meet the ship, feet and heart heavy he walks, his time here is over, and he turns to say goodbye,

But as he turns the scene is gone, alone he stands, and as up the ramp he walks, he emits a heavy sigh.

The Light

Have you've seen the whitest light,
Stood there amongst your long-gone peers,
Or felt the exhilaration of taking flight,
Have you ever heard the whispers in your ears,
Or ever seen your body just lying there,
Yet still been so calm with thoughts so clear,
You know you've died, but you just don't care,
Your body so far away, and yet still so near,
Then back you fall with weightless feeling,
And when you wake, you find your body aches,
Now rest you need to aid in your healing,
Your temperature rises and your body bakes,
The doctor tells you that your still at risk,
You feel like sleeping but fear if you do,
That death may still away with you whisk,
And death will surely come calling for you.
Days go by and he comes for you, but now you're strong,
You understand that he's not your enemy, more like a friend,
He agrees to leave you this time, but for how long,
And he'll greet you again, when your time is finally at end.

The Lonely Parting

Where I walk, I must walk alone,
Sentenced to leave my loving home,
I leave with great sorrow as I still love you so,
Yet I have been called and it's time I must go,
I watch you crying, and it breaks my heart,
That I have been summoned to make a new start,
The life we shared fulfilled me so,
But now it is time for me to go,
One day I'll return to show you the way,
To lead you forward to a brand-new day,
Till then my darling please be aware,
That I will forever love you and always care.

The Mountain

Today I stood upon a mountain top and looked back across the view,

Of places I had been, places I have travelled and skies sometimes grey and stormy but mostly brilliant blue,

I saw the rugged tracks and valleys with rivers long and winding running through,

I remembered times I stumbled and even needed help to stand, but all along I knew,

That this track was unique to me and the pain that I felt was mine and I should never try to hide,

Memories I saw of those that deserted me and those who stood by me,

and those who today still stand loyally by my side,

I looked upon places where I camped by lush green forests and where I didn't seem to have a care,

Ahh but to share it once again with people that I love, and hear again the laughter that filled the air,

I could still make out the sparkling pools of blue where we all would gather and enjoy a drink,

The happy times together when we were all still learning, it seems to quickly that it was over in but a blink.

I could see the times of hardship, the tracks so rugged and so tough and they tested me so,

But looking back there wasn't one period along that track when I thought that I would let go,

I knew my journey that I took was different from other people, and was unique alone to me,

To travel on my own path to experience and see things that no one else could see,

Sure, they would see the sky and touch the earth and feel the wind upon their face,

But just like a recipe, the ingredients we throw in give a very different taste and finish to every place,

I stand here now at the mountain peak and see the path ahead for me from here,

Nothing to fear for it is merely just another track and I'll travel it with no fear,

The distance that I will travel is unknown to me, but that's the way it has always been,

So do not fear the unknown, merely because it's something you have not yet seen,

And whilst my walking may have slowed with age and it may take me a while,

I will start my newest journey not with sorrow or a frown, but a heart filled with a joyful smile.

The Evening Campfire

*I sit and light a fire, for the evening is coming,
and now I must rest,
Behind me a journey that has delivered both the worst,
and the best,
Yet only the memories of good times will I choose to recall,
And I will mark as lessons all the memories of times I did fall,
My life rich in friends and family, and others not known,
I have harvested the rewards of the seeds in
younger days sewn,
A smile taken for payment for a gift of love,
or a favour that I gave,
Or a hand, held out to one who's life from turmoil I did save,
These days I walk slowly, and my body, it grows frail and old,
The warmth once that glowed in my body slowly turns cold,
Yet when the call comes, I am ready, and I'll go with
a smile on my face,
Taking with me memories of love, joy, and of happiness of
this truly beautiful place.*

The Heart Plays On

When forgotten tunes tug on the strings of your heart,
How clearly you hear the music, and then visions start,
Can they just be the memories of the beauty within,
That you instantly recognise and then set free again,
Too long they have been silent, hidden and longing to play,
Free them, let them strum their chords,
to bring happiness I say,
Share it with all in the world that have the ears to hear,
For your beautiful song is nothing to run from or fear,
Let the song in your heart play, be it loud or play it soft,
But allow it to carry all who hear it, up on high aloft,
May your heart always play with such a beautiful beat,
Then let us all sound as one, for the tune will be sweet,
And when my song goes silent and you lay me to rest,
Do not cry or weep, but belt out a song
and give it all your best,
Drink and celebrate and be merry, and beyond
the grave I will hear your sing,
And to my soul and to my memory, greatest joy
and happiness you will bring.

LOVE ABOUNDS

Love Eternal

Take my hand and come walk with me,
Listen to my heart and it will tell thee,
Of what I hold in my heart for you,
The feeling of love so pure and true,
I offer my heart and give it to thee,
Look inside and there you will see,
Both you and I are joined by tether,
That binds us in lasting love forever together,
Then look in my eyes and if you are game,
You will see love that burns eternal as a flame,
Feel my touch and the warmth it does hold,
And let it take away your feeling of cold,
Now hear the words my heart has to say,
Allow them to chase all your fears away,
Finally take my body and join with me,
And let all these things weld to set true love free,
For should come the time when I am no longer there,
My love for you will last eternal, for us to forever share.

A Poem for my Love

Your smile lights my life in every possible way,
And I'm charmed and so love the way that you tease,
and the way you play,
At times your mood can swing from light to a darkness within,
Yet I guarantee you now, my love for you will never dim,
I feel the times when you are lost and times when you're blue,
But these are the times I reinforce, the depths of
my love for you,
There are times you play like a kitten, so playful and so sweet,
And when I try to catch you…you giggle and quickly retreat,
Your eyes sparkle when you smile, and light up every room,
Traversing all spaces, like the smell of the sweetest perfume,
For me you are always beautiful, sweet, and loving and soft,
One touch to my skin sets my heart and soul, soaring aloft,
The love I feel for you grows and knows no boundary or limit,
For every day I am with you passes in what
feels like just a minute,
Soon I will make you my wife, to seal this contract of love
with you,
And together we will sail at the bow of the ship,
gazing at life anew,
There was a time when I may have lost you,
once deep in the past,
But from this moment on I promise that
our love will always last.

For All Mothers

They carry us for months on end,
Their bodies stretching and swelling to amend,
They birth us in sheer exhaustion and pain,
Knowing that their body will never be the same,
They nurse and rear us through sickness and health,
No matter their circumstance be it poverty or wealth,
They wear our bodily fluids, and yet love they still give,
Their hearts still carrying us for as long as they live,
They always try to steer us to be the best we can be,
And guide us to open our eyes when we cannot see,
They are our mothers, and their love lives eternally on,
Even when the time comes, when from her home we have gone,
Her love is eternal, unwavering, and unconditional too,
Regardless of any of the foolish things we do,
So, I take my hat off to all of you mums,
And say thank you on behalf of all daughters and sons,
For the love and caring that you gave and continue to show,
Which even as we age, seemingly continues to grow.

A Star of Light and Love

So sweet and so charming with a soul so soft
Just talking to her can carry you aloft,
A beautiful friend who is ever so true
Give her your trust, and she'll never betray you,
With a ready smile, and ready to help when you ask,
She always remains stoic, yet sweet, and up to the task,
But there are times when she's moody, times when she's blue,
Times when her lights are on, ...but just not for you,
During these times she wears a 1000-yard stare,
When it seems if the world dropped away,
she just wouldn't care,
Is she off fighting her demons in her mind oh so deep,
Or chasing lost memories and dreams to go back and seek,
But she's never gone long, no, she won't allow that,
And as the smile returns, she's always ready to chat,
Jessie, I once told you that you were the best,
That you were so far, far, ahead of the rest,
It took some time to get to know you this well,
But your soul always spoke to me
and through that I could tell,
There are many in this world, that lessons you will teach,
For you are destined for great things, young Jessica Peach,
In your soul burns the light of a magnificent star,
While in your heart you carry great love that will carry you afar
Combined they will lead you to great things that
you'll do and see,
For when a star blends with love there is truly great destiny!

Agape

Let me kiss you gently on your skin and lips,
Whilst I stroke you softly on your breasts, thighs and hips,
Shall I tenderly caress your body till you softly moan,
Make tender love to you while you arch and groan,
Then once you are spent, once you are done,
just lay next to you,
To hold you so dear, to hold you close
and to you alone I'll be true,
Now let me hold you so tenderly, and whisper to you soft,
And then let me take you to the heavens like an angel aloft.

The Journeys End

*I looked in your eyes and saw the reflection of the tears
on my face,*
*You no longer love me, and now you journey off to
a different place,*
*No use trying to ask you to stay or discuss things,
for the feeling is gone,*
*There is nothing for either of us to do anymore,
except now to move on,*
*We walked side by side and hand in hand on this part of
our journey in life,*
*Now we walk in different directions, the bonds we had
sliced with a knife,*
*There are tears in our eyes and we both start our new paths
as we walk away,*
*And whilst I am falling apart inside, I dare not turn back
and beg for you to stay,*
*Thank you for the times we had, and in my memories,
there will always be a part,*
*Glowing bright just for you, there as a reminder,
of the times you held my heart.*

The Greatest Gift

*My children come and join me in this magical place
down at the beach,
Where land meets water and all you ever need is
here in reach,
Walk by my side and let us walk slowly in this golden sand,
Come nearer to me and let me once again hold your hand,
Journey with me toward the horizon and let us slowly walk,
And listen with your heart and not with
your ears as we talk,
Understand that while the sun is still rising high
in the sky for you,
For me is slowly setting and through my eyes
I see a different view,
To me you are still young though I see how much
you've grown,
I watched with pride as you cultivated the seeds of
knowledge that were sown,
Whilst in the distance I also see the ship which
I will board one day to sail away,
Leaving you behind to carry on and pass on your
knowledge to your children one day,
Though I know not when my ship is scheduled
to leave this place,*

*It is important for me to spend some time
and tell you to your face,*

*That I have loved you all with a depth of love that before
I have never known,*

*And the lessons you learnt are still but a fraction of
the lessons I was shown,*

*My children I love you so, and when I go, I leave you one last
thing of value that is true,*

*A heart full of love, a caring soul, and love so great,
made only possible because of you.*

For My Brother

Was many years ago my brother we met through a mutual friend,
Something that turned out to be a blessing that the Universe did send,
Many times, we spent time together making merry in this life,
Hooning around the streets and sometimes getting into strife,
We were brothers not by blood but by bonds that could not be seen,
And it is from those times that our souls melded, never allowing anything in between,
Almost 50 years have passed since the day our journey first did begin,
When the sparks of friendship grew so bright and a brother I did win,
We have shared the path of life together walking by each other's side,
And a love for you grew that burns still bright and I will never hide,
For the love I feel for you runs deep my brother and for you I will always be there,
And the bonds that have grown over the years no outside force will ever tear,
So, brother as we step into the next phase of older age and senior year,
I lift my glass to you and drink to times ahead without any sorrow, regrets or fear,
For you are my true brother and this shall always remain true,
As does the place in my heart where I will always carry my love for you.

Love Is Still Beautiful

What pain love can bring, yet what pain love can heal,
It sends you on high, when someone your heart does steal,
When it ends, and you are unprepared,
how it sends you for a fall,
The impact like running full speed,
headfirst into a brick wall,
Yes, love can be like a cute furry puppy that
suddenly bights,
And at times can leave you crying yourself to
sleep at nights,
But on its return, it comforts you, and offers you healing,
And again, sends you as though you are floating
around the ceiling,
But if there is one thing that I have learnt from love
and can show,
Is that there is truthfully nothing about love,
that I really know,
But love to me is still a beautiful thing to give
and receive and I share it often,
And will continue to do so without fear, till the day,
that I am laid in my coffin.

A Tender Moment Shared for Eternity

Sitting together on the banks of the shore,
Holding the woman I love; I can ask for no more.
The love that I feel fills, and then spills from my heart,
A love that so long ago when we were young did start,
I look into your eyes, and see true love given in return,
For together we feel the heat, as our love does brightly burn,
Your lips meet mine and a tender moment we share,
Washing away all thoughts of worry, sadness or care,
Our hearts beating together, pounding together as one,
Unlike before, this time, from this feeling I will not run,
Wrapped in each other's arms, we watch as night chases the day,
And like stars that sprinkle the sky, forever in my heart you will stay,
I love you so.

Unrequited Love

We never said goodbye and my love never died,
It just wasn't to be at that time, and I took it in my stride,
The day that I left you still burns inside of me,
for the pain ripped me in two,
I loved you so and I never thought I could ever
walk away from you,
Something died that day, and it has never returned to live,
Now I go through the motions, but inside
I have nought to give,
Our letters and our talks, our time we spent connecting,
I live out every day and never stop dissecting,
I don't hate or blame you and I wish you only well.
It was not your fault that my heart so heavily fell,
My chest feels empty now just a huge vacant hole inside,
You still hold my heart, though by now it has surely died,
Sometimes love is like that and leaves us feeling blue,
With thoughts of things that we exchanged
and the moment I met you,
So goodbye my love goodbye and may life be good to you,
I never meant you any harm or to make you blue,
May you find the love and peace you seek one day,
As for me, life goes on and I will keep walking away,
Now with aching heart, and love still burning high,
With heavy heart and tears in my eyes, I finally say goodbye.

A Time Given

There are some people who that believe, there is but one,
Who comes into your life and points your way to the sun.
A person they believe that makes them complete,
The one who'll support them when facing challenge or defeat,
I tell you that you are my angel, my true one and only,
'My forever love', and I know that now, we'll never be lonely,
For you've brought to my life, all your love, all your care,
And it is only when I saw this, that I realized how rare,
It is to meet your angel, your forever lifetime one,
Through your gift of true love, my life has begun,
What you've done, is that you've illuminated my soul,
It's you and your love, that has made me now whole,
The feel of your love, your soft touch and caress,
We're so tight and so close, your heart beats in my chest,
All that we have, has always been missing before,
Though I love you today, tomorrow it will be more,
Our love is our garden, and in it we are the strongest tree,
Which will always grow forever, partly you and partly me,
Darling, you have opened my heart and held it so dear,
Now you are my angel, and I will always keep you near,
Many times, you have seen my highs
and cared when I was low,
For you are my angel, I just need and want you to know,
Once you entered my life, like a ray from the sun up above,
But when we leave, we will leave together in love,
My love for you has become my whole reason to be,
And I hope that in kind, you've found your angel in me.

For My Beautiful Debbie

The joys of love are sometimes just for a moment long,
But the pain of losing love endures your whole life long,
When our eyes kissed and I saw the love in yours shine,
You brought me heaven right there,
when your eyes kissed mine,
This woman I love, loves me as well,
and a world of wonder I see,
A rainbow shines into my heart, because my love, loves me,
One day she may leave me, like a dream that
fades with the dawn,
But her words of love will stay locked in my heart,
my love loves me.

For My Brothers

Many years ago, I started making friends when I was just ten,
We all became best of friends and though I knew it not back then,
Fifty years later despite time and distance we would still be great friends,
And all of us would still get together whenever time lends,
Those precious moments when again we would share,
The friendship and love in our hearts and genuine care,
A brother by blood in my life I have never known,
But seeds of love and friendship in my brother's hearts have grown,
To grow into massive trees that bore great fruit to portion and deal,
Between these brothers for whom so much love and loyalty in my heart I feel,
To Bruce, Neville, David, both Greg's, Steven, Jeff, Robert, Derek, Mark and many more,
Thank you for the journey, the lessons and whatever else may lie in store,
You are all my brothers and there is no price too high for me that I would not pay,
If you ever asked me for anything, I would gladly give it to you today,
Some of you have left to begin a new journey beyond this world,
But we all still carry a part of you in our hearts as you rest in the netherworld,
One day I pray that we'll all get together again, proud, and side by side,
And then off into a brand-new sunrise the valley boys will once again HOON and ride.

Love's Promise

Loving glance, gentle touch, and softest kiss,
She lays her head to his chest in loving bliss,
Embraced in arms that love her so,
She hopes they'll never let her go,
Beating hearts now beating as one,
They carry the rhythm of loves beating drum,
No words are spoken yet communication is there,
Between both hearts as love they share,
Gentle breathing in symmetry with each other,
Loves energy flowing across one another,
For so it is when two hearts in true love do join,
They become as one and for eternity conjoin.

Just another Poem

I loved you so much, I didn't want to let you go,
But though I gave my love fully, yours did not show,
A wall separated our hearts that stretched up to the sky,
I tried to get around but there was no way of getting by,
Looking for a door, but found only windows locked,
All curtains drawn; it seems the view had been blocked,
I felt love for you, and I believed you felt love for me,
Why was it that each other's love we could not see,
I picked up my courage and I walked far away,
But every now and again I still think of you to this day,
Do you ever think of me and what may have been,
If only each other's love, we could have seen,
My love for you never really died,
I would like to think that you never lied,
I love you still, but is that what stops me moving on,
Or has that wall surrounded me, and now love is all gone,
I gave you so much of me, including my heart,
But like everything else you still have that part...!
If you still have it, then there's no need to now send it back,
For if you open the box, you'll find it shrivelled and black.
There you'll also find a knife still buried deep,
One I put there myself when your love I could not keep,
Just one last thing if you don't mind,
Return my knife if you could be so kind?

Merry Christmas and Love to All

*They say that Christmas is a time of joy,
a time of love and sharing,
A time of the year when we are urged to extend
the loving hand of caring,
This I do today amongst you all, my family,
and my friends as we all gather here,
First please lift your glass and drink with me, long and
deep, to a very heartfelt cheer,
May each and all of you know the depth of love that
I am blessed to have known,
And the love I have in my heart that grows from
the seeds that each of you have sown,
Today I give to you love from my heart, all the love I hold,
and I share this with you,
But be warned that if you accept this gift in full,
then something will happen to you too,
For unlike material gifts that are finite in their use,
love has no start, and has no end,
Love once planted, continues to grow and those who
cultivate love, its gifts will send,
I ask that you please accept my love
and the spirit in which I give,
May you know the peace that love can bring,
and the rewarding life that you can live.*

Ode to Women

In this journey I have known women at varying stages of my life,
From friend to mother and sister, and once I even took one for my wife,
Though the marriage did not last, we have remained friends so true,
And still have time to share or help each other when one of us is blue,
Others I have had relations with, but all have played their special part,
For I have loved them all, and they all still live in my heart,
There were times of sadness, times when we argued so,
But memories of happier times are only what I know,
Some have been lovers and others I know only as a friend,
But to all the women in my life, a heartfelt thank you I do send,
I know I've not always been easy and at times I was just a pain,
I'm sure at times it even felt to you like I was sending you insane,

I still know most of you, and you all remain still in my heart,

For varying reasons each one, even though we are now apart,

No need to hate or distance us just because the love is gone,

We played the part in each other's life, and it was just time to move on

Women have taught me of love and how to show it, and not to hide,

What I felt for others from the love that lives in me so deep inside,

For women are beautiful creations of strength and love and wonder,

And those who underestimate them will most certainly be torn asunder.

The Loving

In the darkness they lay silent, together close in bed,
He spooned into her back, softly kissing her head,
Gently his fingertips lightly run over her soft, porcelain skin,
She begins quivering with delight, hoping he would soon begin,
But he wishes not to be rushed, for him her body was new,
And there were places to explore, as his member grew,
She reached back and held it, and felt the blood in it pound,
As he gently kissed her stomach,
and then moved down to her mound,
He caressed her body, slowly exploring every part,
She felt his throbbing member enter her,
and the pounding of his heart,
His hand moved down again to caress her bodies
womanly fold,
Touching it so lightly, as she trembled in his hold,
Nibbling at her neck and ear, and whispering things so sweet,
They would soon both erupt in passion,
in an explosion of love and heat,
She feels the passion building and arches her back to moan,
He feels that moment coming, and thrusts deep into her zone,
She rolls slowly onto her back, exhausted but feeling fully sated,
For this was the kind of passion, that she had
so long for waited,
He moved up toward her, and held her close to him
while they lay,
Laying together for hours they snuggled,
and slowly drifted away.

When Souls Connect

Conversation flows like fine sparkling wine,
While discussion moves on to a previous time,
Fine food is consumed with elegant haste,
Savoured with glee, good company adds to the taste,
Laughter and joy resonate through the air,
While the sweet taste of friendship takes away all care,
But for now, we sit with not a care in the world,
Gone the memories of problems that against us were hurled,
A genuine connection with true friends and soul mates,
Who all have in some way seen the great pearly gates,
But they sent us all back for they all knew,
We'd take over the place if they let this mob through,
So here we sit together in a tavern enjoying a meal,
As deep in discussion and valuable time we steal,
Hearts forever connected in friendship and trust,
And so it shall be even after we have all returned to dust.

LIFE'S LESSONS

For the Troubled

*Look for those lost through this poets' eyes,
Listen to them and their mournful cries,
Sad they are not, they are just tired and lost,
Beaten by life and paying a terrible cost,
Surrounded by fog and unable to see,
Please listen to them and hear their plea,
Listen not with your ears for these they'll deceive,
But listen with your heart and you'll hear them grieve,
Turn them to the light and lead them away from the dark,
Away from a world for them so bleak and so stark
Aim them to light and try not to judge,
But start them moving with a gentle nudge,
They seek not attention, nor ask for your pity,
Lost in their mind, with more voices than a committee,
I ask, please love one another and watch for those troubled,
Because for some, every day their problems seem doubled,
Love can be the answer, and love for them will save,
And thank you to those who listened or gave.*

For My Dear Friend

Lift the veil that covers your eyes, and return where you belong,
Allow the mist to lift and clear your eyes to see, for the place you are is wrong,
Lift the mists of deceit and deception that blurs your view of life,
Your world has turned upside down as you find your life in strife,
You struggle to see that in which you are stuck, staring into the haze,
Times of not leaving your home for weeks or even just sometimes days,
Cast off the pains they set upon you, please leave them far behind,
And come back to the world where thoughts are clear and kind,
You are missed and still loved by all, and we await your welcome return,
Come back my friend, and from those who wronged you, away you must turn,
For we are all waiting here to welcome you, to share a drink and hear your views,
To welcome you with open arms my friend, and gladly chase away your blues.

A Poem for our War Heroes

He stared across the open field, his eyes are wet with tears,
He remembers the fighting, the blood, the screaming,
and all the fears,
He thinks of those that lost their lives that day,
in battle so fierce and hard,
How every step was measured, in desperate efforts to gain
that extra yard
He remembers the look of those he killed,
and the horror in their eyes,
As their life was taken from them for
the sake of greed, land and lies,
The smell of death still lingers for him,
forever in his nose,
A smell that haunts him to this day
and in his face, it shows
How long he has sought the peace that so
eludes him to this day,
The war is over now they said, and then simply sent
him on his way,
Yet a ticking bomb inside his head, he knew not
how to defuse,
What life now awaits me, he thought,
what life can I now choose?
So, he wandered lonely for many years,
just living day to day,
Living with nightmarish memories in his head,
that just would not go away,
Was he really such an evil man, or was fighting for his
country actually the error?

*Now his travels have brought him to the place,
where all his nightmares began,*

*Back to the time where he killed, his first victim,
a poor unfortunate man,*

He cried as he buckled, and went through his knees in pain,

*And laid roses for the memories, of all the men
who he had slain,*

*Now it is time he quietly murmured, and laid down
on the grass,*

*And in that moment, he finally found his peace
as he felt his life force pass.*

PT8D

Worlds colliding, crashing and burning as violence wins again,
Thoughts erupting, so much turmoil trying to send me insane,
Memories blending, smashing and making conflicts anew,
Causing thoughts so deep, so sullen and oh so very blue,
Spiraling down in my mind, feeling totally out of control,
As deeper down I fall, uncontrollably into this black hole,
Voices all screaming as one at me deep inside of my head,
Wounds are opened as old demons once again are fed,
They rule for now but not for long, for soon again I know,
I will regain control and win, and away they will once more go,
Leaving me battered, bruised, and alone, to rebuild once more,
In my mind now filled with blood, with damage and with gore,
Such is life when you struggle with torrid events of the past,
Where memories of horrors seen, seem too constantly last,
We learn to live with these traumatic moments of relapse,
But I believe one day, there will come a time when perhaps,
Calm I hopefully will find, and love and peace will be the norm,
And my ship will finally find the calm that follows from a storm.

Heartache

Have you ever felt the sting of love unrequited,
Or lost your love when along the journey they alighted,
Maybe the cold hand of death whisked them away,
Or maybe they just told you they just couldn't stay,
No matter how you lost your love, the pain is still the same,
It leaves you distraught, and your heart
it will strike and maim,
Taking no prisoners and leaves only a gnawing pain,
To those who have experienced it, they're never the same,
Much later you'll think back and remember the highs,
But when it first happens, you'll just hear their
echoed goodbyes,
Your chest has been gutted and the pain burns down deep,
Eyes cried dry with no tears left to shed,
yet you continue to weep,
And you cannot help but wonder when
the pain you feel will ever end,
When will you allow yourself to forget so that
your heart can finally mend,
But till then you hide it inside and you carry
a smile to your friends,
Whilst in private times you cry, wondering when it all ends,
You dare not show or let anyone see the pain that you carry,
There was a time when you both had plans that you'd marry,
But all that is gone now, torn away, and you feel ripped apart,
Whilst at night you lay there in bed, alone,
nursing your broken heart.

The Black Dog

*Ever noticed when the curtain around you
is slowly being drawn?
Your mood has gone from a sense of high to
a familiar feeling of forlorn,
The ground beneath you now, somehow no longer
seems to be so firm,
You try to hide and keep still, but in fact all
you can do is squirm,
You smell the stench in your nose that is so familiar to you,
The odour that you know so well, for you this is not new,
You know you cannot outrun it, it would be just
a futile attempt,
For tonight I feel, that from his teeth you will not be exempt,
You smell his foul breath and then feel his teeth
ripping at your flesh,
The painful sting as he sinks them in makes
you twitch and thresh,
A voice in your head is telling you that it is better
to just let him win tonight,*

*That it is better just to lay down and die
and let him claim this fight,*

*But your survival fight kicks in,
and you turn to face him down,*

*You rally your strength, and with your
fists flailing on him you, "go to town",*

*He reels back as you land a blow
and dislodge his painful bight,*

*Yelping and barking from shock,
he slowly backs away from this fight,*

*You have won once again but you know
it is only just for another day,*

*Slowly he backs away to whence he came,
beaten this time at his own game today,*

*In the shadows of your mind though he skulks,
and lurks, always living there,*

*Waiting for another chance to pounce again
and at your emotions to tear.*

My True Demon

*Recently I was walking through my mind, through its
corridors and rooms, just enjoying the view,*

*It is something that I will do from time to time,
just to review what I have been through,*

*I looked back on so many memories, of lessons learnt,
some good, some hard,*

*But as I went down deeper, I found a room that
I had locked and barred,*

*The noises that echoed from there made the hair stand
on my neck,*

*Then I saw the key hanging and wondered,
do I have the courage this room to check?*

*Slowly then I turned each of the locks,
and swung away the heavy iron gate,*

*As I reached for the final handle a blood curdling scream
erupted and I paused and wondered my fate,*

*Slowly then I cracked the door and took
a sneaky look inside,*

*And what I saw made me fall to me knees
and my tears I could not hide,*

*Locked inside I saw the torments of previous years
and the pain I grew to know,*

I stood frozen in horror as I watched the crescendo of the torture giver grow,

For here was the demon that had manipulated me until the day I fought back and deftly won,

Not only defeating him but locking him away in this darkened gloomy room to wait for death to come,

But none of this is what made me crumble, no, for I had long before my triumphant battle song sung,

It was the demon himself that made me crumble, but not in fear or pain or regret at what I had done,

For as he moved into the light, I saw him for as he was, and it chilled me to the bone, calling on my frozen legs to flee,

As the demon I had locked away all those years ago moved to face me I hast watched and as our eyes met I recognized the demon, and the demon, it was…me.

Abused

Tormented by past abuse she sits and wanders through the corridors of her mind,
Searching for that room or quiet corner in which to hide, yet she struggles so to find,
Still blaming herself for what others took from her as a child,
Memories of abuse from others who are rightfully so reviled,
Nights she lives with the nightmares of the past and days are just a struggle,
In a never-ending loop of thoughts that she constantly must juggle,
Thoughts of death and suicide have taken her many times to the edge,
Standing there whilst contemplating of jumping from that ledge,
But that would be giving in to the scum and filth who should be dead,
Who deserve a tormented death for how she often was ripped and bled,
With thoughts of feeling you are not worthy and somehow it was your fault,

Your mind constantly trapped in vicious battles of war internally you have fought,

You are not to blame sweet one, for the acts that almost sent you insane,

I only hope and pray that time and love will help you learn to cope with the pain,

Allowing you to move on and live your life with happiness and love and begin to mend,

To accept you are worthy, and that people still love you, and always will till the end.

Wisdom Shunned

I've fallen into the water, and I am surrounded by fog,
I must have slipped and fallen, running from the black dog,
Normally I would start to swim back for the shore,
But this time I'm lost, and bruised, battered and sore,
What sin have I done to deserve to be left out in this cold,
When in truth the only reality is that I got old,
I try to go on, but things are getting out of hand,
With a mist that surrounds me, taking away all view of land,
Every day I tread water, till today I realized with a shudder,
That I'm like a ship adrift on an ocean with no rudder,
Others kick me aside and forget of my knowledge,
You've obviously learnt it all when you went to your college,
But I will drift on my back patiently,
till the tides free me once more,
For either I'll sink to the bottom, or float back to shore,
One way or another, I will find my way back,
To walk again on my own unique track,
And you may look down at me because you think
you know it all,

When you don't see ahead your own imminent fall,
But unlike you I'll still help you stand again,
Brushing you off, and then giving advice
to deal with the pain,
For that is who I am, and I cannot nor will not change me,
And you are who you are, and this is how it must be,
For your path is not mine nor mine is for you,
But together we are part of this beautiful world us two,
I do not blame others for the fault lies in me,
Where I cast my eyes and what I choose to see,
So now I divert my eyes from all that is glum,

The Tormented Soldier

Standing in the dark always searching for light,
To fill his thoughts and take away this endless night,
Lost deep somewhere in the shadows of his mind,
Though answers he seeks, these he still cannot find,
Peace always seems to be just too far away,
"Be happy that you returned alive", he can still hear the say,
His mind returns to a simpler time when he stood in the sun,
To a time before he was taught how to fight with a gun,
When life was easy and laughter flowed free,
When life's path was clear as far as he could see,
Then he gave of himself to fight in war
and pick up the sword,
An adventure he thought to defeat the enemy abroad,
But the adventure turned sour, and his days turned
dark and bleak,
Then when he returned of these he could not speak,
But tonight, he found peace sitting in an armchair
in his home,
In darkness he sat like so many times before all alone,
When there came a visitor to see him and take away
his torment,

And lead him off to peace that was truly heaven sent,
When they found him, the next day sitting there alone in his place,
They could not understand the peaceful look on his face,
Gone was the tormented look in his eyes,
Gone were the lines in his face from his endless cries,
He seemed to be smiling some even said,
This soldier had found peace and grew wings and his torment he shed,
His sacrifice was great and the price he paid high,
God bless you soldier, thank you, and rest now in peace as you fly.
And follow your lighthouse, till you have found true peace too.

The Unknown Reality

I sit alone and try to find the calm to so many things as my mind drifts away, and slowly I go numb,

With futile thoughts I try to catch each moment as I find myself travelling within myself once more,

Exploding into a void where nothing around me seems real anymore and I am in between worlds again,

Like looking through windows, no pain, no sorrow, just a vague curiosity, I feel lost, maybe some sleep will help,

Life is now so surreal and yet it is these moments that I feel so aware and realize what we should all fear,

I look back on the times when emotion was too much and we found ourselves screaming for help, either in mind in reality,

But now you feel nothing, only memories playing like movie reels past the windows in your mind gliding by,

No forward, no back, no up or down, and no consequence or fear, in this moment I am lost to all,

I stop and stare at the scenes that play out in front of me in wonder, I am alone in the vastness of this place,

Tomorrow I will wake once more, and this moment will have been just like a scene from a dream,

Then with feet again firmly planted in the so-called reality of here and now I will venture out once more,

Till again this place that I visit calls on me once more beckoning me to stay, but then I wonder, maybe it is actually here that I visit and observe, and where I come to play?

A True Hero

You went away to fight a war,
But at this country's heart it tore,
There were those who would oppose,
And in the streets the riots rose,
But you were proud to go and fight,
To defend us all and shine the light,
The light that was to guide ones like me,
For without men like you I would never see,
I have always been thankful to the men that did go,
Who suffered so much for people you don't even know,
Some came back scarred on their bodies and mind,
Whilst some never came back, and were left behind,
Others paid the ultimate price with their lives,
Leaving grieving family, girlfriends, and wives,
You came back and served us once again,
Upon your return for the Police Force you did train,
But now your retired peace you seek, and you just keep going,
Whilst the seeds of love in you just keep growing,
You are now a light for the weak and the lost,
For those whose minds have sometimes become crossed,
Lost in places that no one would want to trek,
But you go in there and to guide them back,
God Bless you and thank you my dear friend,
For the love you show knows truly no end,
Your heart is full of love and overflows with kind,
Whilst helping the folks with left with tortured mind.

Empty Words

It's amazing in conversation what can be heard,
When you listen for the unspoken word,
Like watching a target floating in the sky,
Around it somehow the arrows will fly,
You listen intently but still do not hear,
For the words are stuck in their throats with fear,
Do they think that I will scream and shout,
When their true thoughts are finally let out,
Or do they think that I just don't see,
The game that they are playing with me,
I play along and they think they have won,
But it is I who hold the smoking gun,
What use are words when the truth is not spoken,
When words without meaning are the only token,
Like empty vessels they amplify,
The words that from their mouths do fly,
So, I rise and thank them for the words they say,
And as I wander off from them, far away,
I think how sad it must be,
To speak so much, but not feel free.

Hidden Scars

Tear the skin and break the bone,
Smash the body till you scream and groan,
All will heal with proper care,
They leave a scar, no matter there,
But torment the soul and fry the mind,
Twist your thoughts, till sanity is left behind,
No easy fix no bandage will shield,
The pain you feel from the thoughts you yield,
Run from the thoughts that poison your brain,
Or stand paralysed and frozen in pain,
Nobody sees the thoughts in your head,
Unlike a wound that has opened and bled,
You carry on never willing to share,
The pain you carry and the burden you wear.

In Dark, Lost and Lonely

You lay there in the darkness of your mind,
Your eyes twitch watching your life unwind,
I call your name, yet you barely hear,
Your gaze is fixed and frozen in fear,
The phone rings but you dare not answer the call,
For fear it may cause you again, to spiral and fall,
Lost to this world, lost to this dimension,
You're lost in your mind in a sideshow extension,
So come to my heart and there rest true,
Please allow me to help, heal, and nurture you,
Bring you back and reclaim what was yours,
To lock away these demons behind stronger doors,
So, rest my dear friend here deep in my heart,
For tomorrow we'll begin on a brand-new start.

The Battle

I am weary, I am tired, and I am sore from the fight,
Scars and wounds testify to the veracity of my fight,
I stand amongst the scattered remains,
of what was once my old life,
And look ahead to the new road to be carved
yet with sword and knife,
My colleagues fought beside me this time,
so valiant and so true,
Like legendry Aussie troopers, we banded together
for this great blue,
Ahead of us awaits the spoils of our hard-fought win,
Yet for me, wealth was not the reason that
I started this great din,
For the price that I have paid, for me has been quite high,
This battle was not just for me but also others in mind, and
was to win or die,
For I have had my time and, in my life, experienced it all,
From cheering to remorse, sometimes
I lost, other times I stood tall,
But now that I am older, the welfare of my children is
my only concern,
And with them in my mind and heart, I faced the battle
again to take one final turn,
One last roll of the dice, one last push, one more gamble for
my goal to accrue,
Only this time my nerve in battle will be rewarded
and my arrow fly straight and true.

Pure Love Misunderstood

So, you think that I want you for gain,
and that I don't really care,
You think that my kindness brings expectation,
from you something to share,
I want nothing from you but to help you,
and make you feel good,
The way that you are meant to, the way I feel you should,
Life can be full of misery and into our life pain does weave,
My kindness is merely my attempt to give you a reprieve,
Those who come across my path, and in them a need I feel,
To share a kind or tender word, which may help
them to heal,
Yet you still do not believe that I do this without wanting gain,
That somehow, I will try to fill your world with
sorrow or shame,
But I assure you, it is merely an act of kindness,
an act of caring,
Because the love in my heart was only ever meant for sharing,
I am sorry that you have never been given or felt pure
love before,
And that you thought that all I wanted was to get
a foot into your door,
I will say what I need to and hopefully you will hear,
and then I'll walk away,

And hopefully it will sink in and some of what I have said
will help your day,
But if you still refuse me, please do not try to follow
or enter my walls,
Or walk through my mind and hear their thoughts echo
in the long empty halls,
With locked rooms either side filled with boxes where
I hide away my pain,
And memories inside of them that would send those not
as strong insane,
Or switch on the light to places that keep constantly
in the dark,
Where memories that have pained me,
I have chosen those to park,
Share a kind word if you want to thank me,
but please then let me be,
My love to you is honest, but better still, it is given for free.

Mistakes or Lessons

*Like a loop of film playing over and over,
screening in my mind,
So many things I think I would have changed back then,
if only I had known,
The things that still torment me,
that I have tried to leave behind,
Memories of moments in my mind,
that have engorged and grown,
Times of acting like a man of steel,
where compassion should have been,
Other times of running away, from decisions that
had to be made,
If only then the outcome of my actions,
and the impact I could have seen,
I may have made them differently,
and these current memories would fade,
But what would they be replaced with,
what scenario would have done,
Trading one bad memory for another,
in the many scenarios in my mind,
The outcome would not have changed, and my actions
I would still seem dumb,
So, the guilt lives on and there is nothing to do but
accept it and leave the past behind.*

Reflections of Self

I scream and shout, yet my mouth does not move,
I long for something my soul to sooth,
Falling so fast and cannot stop,
Speeding downward on this endless drop,
Drowning in an ocean of a bottomless hell,
Yet no one else can see this, and I will not tell,
Outside I seem so calm so peaceful and kind,
While deep inside is a tormented and tortured mind,
Talk to me as you will, and I will respond in same,
Whilst deep down, inside I hide all my pain,
There before me, alone, I see myself stand,
Looking back in anger with threatening clenched hand
Eternal in battle, I prepare to face off with me,
In a battle that no one else, but only I can see.

My Journey

I tried walking away from my pain, but then I just found more,
I walked even further away and from ones I loved I tried to lock the door,
Still, it made no difference and the pain it was still there,
So, I ran as fast as I could, even further, to stay away from all who care,
Here I was alone and surrounded by those that I did not know,
But the pain still did not stop, in fact it just seemed to grow,
I cried and wept and with sullen look upon my face I looked up to the sky,
Oh Lord why did you do this to me, what have I done, please tell me why,
To my amazement a voice came back, and it was soft, and caring, and called me son,
He said son I have been calling you back since before you started to run,
You chose not to hear me, and you ignored me when again, I did call,
You even ignored me when you stumbled, and had a mighty fall,
But I am patient and loving, and am here for you to show and guide you the way,

*For you took off in the wrong direction,
which led you to where you are today,*

*Take my hand my child and together we will take
this journey that you walk,*

*I will guide you, hold you, and carry you if needed,
and as we go we can talk,*

*He led me back to friends and family, and the strangers to
me became known,*

*Pain then started subsiding, and remarkably where was
hate, I found love had grown,*

*The pain also gave way to wondrous feelings of love,
caring and goodwill,*

*Which I have added to my belongings now, and in others
I seek to instil,*

*But the greatest thing He taught me was that love is
the answer, and love is the key,*

*When you carry love in your heart, your path, and the love
in others, will be laid out clearly to see.*

HEALING

Words of Love and Understanding

When you read this, you will know I am talking to you,
Lay down your worries, your pain and your fears
and rest in my heart,
You feel that no one understands, yet I understand you
and your needs all too well,
You feel like you're alone, despite those around you,
You feel unloved, despite the words of those
who tell you that they love you,
You feel worthless despite your true value,
Come and rest in my arms and in my heart.
Allow me to give you a hand and help you.
Not for reward but, merely out of love.
You are beautiful and worthwhile, though you do not see it.
So, lay down your burdens, and come and rest in my heart
Love one another and show them in kind,
And look for love from others, do not be blind,
Love like time is eternal you see,
And does not die like you or me,
There will always be some in your life who will do you wrong,
Forgive them and with love in your heart send them along,
Harbor no hate in your heart nor your soul,

Please do not allow hatred to take its toll,
For time will heal and love will ease all pain,
Through showing this love we can only gain,
Enjoy every day, remember it could always be worse,
And whether or not you take heed now of my little verse,
It does not matter, for I am planting a seed,
That one day may sprout root, and others will take heed,
At the beauty once planted that will now be in full flower
And love will be seen, as this woman or man's greatest power

An Old Mans Wisdom

I listened to an old man today, as he spoke to me of many times in his life,
Times in his youth and other playful times, and the time when he took a wife,
Of times of horrendous loss, times of grief, and times when he was so lost,
The times when decisions he made, delivered consequences at far too great a cost,
Other times when ending it all, seemed to be the only path to follow,
Whilst trying to combat and conquer the feelings he held inside, the empty, the dark and the hollow,
Times of sheer happiness and joy, of love, of happiness, and times of wealth and gain,
Followed by times of poverty, depths of sadness and loss, all filled with so much pain,
He told me of the times when he wandered through this life, not knowing where to go,
Which directions he should follow, or what decisions to make, or how he would ever know?
It all seemed to him that he just rambled through life blind, and he never had a plan,
Stumbling through this life, many times feeling empty, like a lost and lonely man,

But in the end, he quietly said, you do the best you can, and that is all that you can do,

Believe in the decisions you have made for this path, and the lessons sent, for they were laid just for you,

Then he looked knowingly at me, gave me a nod, and told me that he hoped he made things clearer,

And I walked away from him with tears in my eyes and realized that I had been talking to a mirror.

Reaching Out

You feel the emptiness deep within that you cannot hide,
That gnawing pain that eats away at you so deep inside,
The type that makes you wish that sometimes you could die,
Pain that may make others take their life,
or at the very least try,
I ask you, how can I help you my friend, to take this pain away?
To help you realize that it is still so worthwhile to stay,
So let me lend an ear to you, to hear your troubled word,
Allow me to let me let you know that someone
at least has heard,
Let me stay and talk with you and allow me now to share,
Words straight from my heart to let you know that
I really care,
For you my friend, are ever so dear to me,
It is only your happiness that I long to see,
But should you leave, should you follow through,
You should also know that I will always love you,
No judgement passed, no threats of hell do I send,
Just love from me to you my friend, until the very end,
So come to my side dear friend, and let us gently walk,
And allow me to listen, while you just talk.

My Offer

*Have you ever seen the darkness,
Or heard yourself silently cry,
Felt the cold freeze of hate toward you,
Or heard as you let out a sorrowed sigh,
You are not alone my friend,
For I will be there by your side,
To support you in your time of need,
As from this world we sometimes hide.*

A Different Way of Thinking

Why do you seek the evil and sadness when there is so much beauty that surrounds?

Turn your head and look around you and you will see what beauty truly abounds,

You sit there and struggle and wonder why you cannot shake the blues,

Yet every night you tune into the evil and pain streamed over the evening news

You complain to others that life for you is so hard, and yet you will not change your way,

Wanting things to change, yet you continue to go about your life doing the same thing every single day,

I do not chastise you, and please forgive me if it may seem this is what I am doing to you,

Please I ask you to walk with me for a little while and join me as I journey to seek what is true,

Leave behind the illusions of what is fed to you, and break free from the constant lies, and then run,

Start a journey to find yourself and know what this life holds for you be free from existence so glum,

Find the peace within yourself and know that you are beautiful, loved and worthwhile,

Learn that beauty comes from within and not from high cheekbones, clear skin or latest fashion style,

Feel free to express what lies within for it is your journey, and it is unique to you alone, so do not be meek like a mouse,

But shine for all your worth, because whilst the ignorant may look and scoff, for others you will be their lighthouse,

Do not criticise others just because you don't understand, but listen to their story and you will start to know,

That we all seek the same thing, we all have the same goal, of people understanding us, and through this we can grow,

Love my friend is the answer, and love can cure all, but first you need to love yourself,

And only once you have truly mastered this,

then you can spread love's true wealth.

A New Start

*One day I awoke and found that the light was gone,
and I was left in the dark,*

*In a tunnel of black where light did not enter in this place,
so cold to my heart,*

*I stumbled to feel my surrounds, trying to find something
that was familiar to me,*

*Straining my eyes, I refused to believe that the light had
just gone, but there was nothing I could see,*

*I remember I fell and felt the pain of my conceived failure,
and it hurt more than the fall,*

*I cried long and hard and thought that all was lost,
but eventually fighting back I stood tall,*

*Lost for a familiar point to head, I looked towards the
heavens to give me direction,*

*And as I slowly turned and felt my way, I headed off
feeling as if I had made a connection,*

*Then to my surprise a point of light did appear before me,
and broke the dark in this place,*

*And a warm burst of wind cleansed the foul air,
and seemed to softly caress my face,*

I stumbled closer to the light, falling once again for my journey was still not done,

But my pace was certainly quickening now, to a point where I could almost run,

I broke into the sunshine, and it streamed over my body, my heart, and my soul,

Again, I could see direction, and once again I felt as though I was whole,

For there before me I saw skies so blue, and scenery that just left me in awe,

And triumphantly I looked up to the heavens and gave thanks for the new future that I saw.

From True Love Born

Your screams of pain I hear across the distance and through the night,
So much pain I feel that arises from your memories of your constant mental fight,
Consequences I see of the words that cut you, leaving you bleeding and scarred,
The bitterness in your soul I taste and understand that for you, now to trust is now hard,
Your flickering light has led me to you so I may reach out and offer you hope,
Not to slap you down, or challenge you or taunt you, nor do I wish to provoke,
Merely to help to heal and lift you, guide you back to the person you could be now,
Not back to who you were, that person is gone, filled of hate and pain, and blind to see,
But the person that is evolving, like a phoenix, will be reborn to live once more,
Much wiser and filled with love and forgiveness, so much more than any time before,
That chapter of pain, is now merely a memory, come and take my hand and follow me,
Let me take you to your place of rebirth, where you can finally meet your true destiny.

Agape Love

*Lay down your worries, your pain, and your fears,
and rest in my heart,*
*You feel that no one understands, yet I understand you
and your needs all too well,*
Though you feel like you're alone despite those around you,
*And you still feel unloved despite the words of those
who sprout their love,*
You feel utterly worthless despite your great value,
*So, I invite thee to come and rest in my arms
and find solace in my heart,*
Let me help you and guide you to make a new start,
*Not for gifts in return or monetary reward,
but merely from love,*
*You are beautiful and worthwhile, even though
you do not see it,*
*So lay down your sword, and again I invite you to come
and rest in my heart.*

Hidden Rooms

Wandering through the hallways and rooms of my mind,
I really cannot be sure of what I am trying to find,
To taste again the succulence of life that so excited me once,
Trying to find what I have not experienced in many, many months,
Seeking out the crevices, where my deepest memories live,
To feel them once more, in an attempt for my life meaning to give,
Do I visit and troll the wrong places, am I so lost in the past,
Or should I move forward now, and set the sails to my mast,
Shall I let the wind blow this ship to places not yet found,
To play the songs of life and create a new musical sound,
Or do I stay in the comfort of these things that I knew,
Stick to thoughts and memories that fit me like an old shoe,
For the first time in my life is it true that I am scared to move on,
To try that new exotic taste or to sing along to that new song,
Is it really time for me to dock and stop sailing this ship,
To run her aground as though she's sailed her final trip,

*I wonder if these are the questions that go through minds of all?
Is it normal to find that suddenly your life seems to stall?
Where do I find the key to the ignition to again excite and start,
The things that used to pump the adrenalin and excite my heart,
Not knowing the answers, I now set my sail and point my ship to sea,
I know not where the wind or currents on this journey will take me,
And I pray what I find will be the things that I seek and long for,
But I know I won't find it going back to hidden rooms, to open an old memories door.*

Catching the Wind

How do you hold a memory in your hand?
Or permanently write a message in the sand?
What if you could catch the wind that carries a thought?
Do you remember the smell of the first car you bought?
What about the touch so soft and sweet of the first lips
you ever did kiss?
Do you remember the feel of your first love so true?
Or are you just looking blankly, thinking I haven't a clue?
What about making love with the first person for whom
you really cared?
The first time you wanted to make sure,
that the orgasm was shared.
So many memories I remember,
and yet so many I have lost,
Some matter little, yet others are forgotten
at a far greater cost,
Our memories are precious, and each have
a taste of their own,
They are there to remind us of the lessons
we have been shown,
Sometimes I admit I would love to go back to
a memory of mine,
Like Groundhog Day and relive that moment by going
back in time,
For me I would relish to sit there with those
I have loved and have lost,
Something I would gladly pay handsomely for,
regardless of the cost.

Lessons

*At last, my arrow right on target now has hit,
The darkness that was once so bleak, now is lit,
And I look towards a new future looking bright,
To stride ahead with heart and soul full of light,
No simple task, no easy fix, it required patience and work,
To overcome the obstacles that always seemed to lurk,
And as for these hard times, through which I once fought,
I'd like to thank them all, for the lessons they taught.*

Deaf Ears Will Hear

Wise words in time will all fall away,
Lost in memories and then washed away,
Now lessons we learnt are lost in time,
The fact they're forgotten such a terrible crime,
Words of knowledge that once rang true,
Fall on the on deaf ears on those with no clue,
Whilst the meaning ripped asunder that once could save,
The ones who would listen and dare be so brave,
To stand before all and raise their spirited sword,
Of people amassed and starting the hoard,
But what use are words when the message they won't heed,
As the masses go on to reopen wounds that continue to bleed,
There are some who find the light of way,
Who continue to preach and replace the night with day,
Whilst trying to stand and to spread the light,
They defy the hordes and spearhead the fight,
Enlightened are they and wisdom they know,
Listen to them and the knowledge will flow,
Throw away your conceptions of religion and faith,
They will only bring you opposing fury and wraith,
To be enlightened you must first understand,
And be guided by the lessons when they take you by hand,
You won't learn it all in a single lesson or two,
But open your heart each day to the lessons anew,
For one day you will understand just why we are here,
And this knowledge you learn will remove you from fear.

Criticism

*You're mistaken, for no need have I to answer to you,
For things that I've done, or things that I do,
So, what if I've lived my life the way that I did,
While you run and you hide, and cower in fear,
But come and let us talk, let me buy you a beer,
Whilst I will not feel guilty or wear your blame,
I will share some stories and maybe wisdom you'll gain,
What you see in me, and what I see in you,
Are paramount for the survival of us two,
What one creates as waste may be useful for the other,
And in all truth, in this world, I am still your brother,
Not by blood, or by family bonds, but joined by much more,
Joined by the energy that lives deep at our core,
So, judge me not for our differences that push us apart,
And look for the love instead, that joins us by our heart.*

An Angel Sings

The music starts, let the performance begin,
To say she merely sings would surely be a sin,
Her voice so pure, it just carries you away,
So, let the journey begin as realty fades from my day,
My world begins to change shape, shifting of sorts,
My mind is filling with dreams and fresh thoughts,
The clouds roll around, and the wind it does blow,
Even light becomes magical, and my senses all glow,
Her voice so captivating, and her beauty is timeless,
While her svelte body shimmers in a long flowing dress,
I am totally captivated by the performance she gives,
Floating afar in my mind where imagination lives,
Then she sings a verse, and it hits me hard in my chest,
Making an impact so much more powerful than the rest,
Inside my body she somehow caresses my heart,
Unleashing emotions that now fly like a dart,
Shooting wildly, enjoying their new freedom in flight,
Unlocked from the gloom where they were hidden in night,
Free now to see the beauty of day,
No longer pained by those gone away,
Emotions unlock, and my heart is set free,

*I watch as my heart spirals towards the sky with such glee,
I fly like a bird and then run like a racehorse,
No burdens I feel as I shed all feelings of remorse,
The world looks so beautiful down there below,
All this from listening to your remarkable show,
But your show it is ending, and in mind and body I'm spent,
Emma, you carried me, and I am glad that I went,
Thank you, Emma for the journey you gave,
A reprieve from this world where I feel sometimes a slave.*

My Gift

If I could grant one wish for you,
Would you ask for yourself a possession that's new,
Or maybe you'd ask for world peace today,
Or that all the worlds' cancers be taken away,
Maybe you would request and end to all war,
Or to feed the starving with their stomachs so sore,
What if I just made everyone smile,
Wouldn't that be lovely just for a while,
If I could take away the pain that makes people cry,
Would you let me grant you this wish,
or would you still ask me why,
I will tell you this with heart pure and true,
If it brought peace to the world, then there is nothing I won't do,
If it was in my power to ever grant this wish, I would try,
Even if it meant that in the process I'd surely die,
Remember something please, if you can for just a while,
To share your love with others, and try to make them smile,
Maybe sometimes tell someone who needs to hear that they're quite unique,
In a world where so many people, anonymity they seek,
Give love as the answer to questions like, why are we here,
Offer help to those people that live constantly in fear,
Help spread love and caring and hopefully one day,
Together as a team, we'll all make pain, greed and hate go away.

Coloured People

Are you a person of colour, maybe various shades of grey,
Maybe you have green eyes and envy is your way,
Or are you blue deep down within and never laugh or smile,
Maybe you are in the pink and smiling all the while,
What if yellow is your colour and you brighten every day,
But then do not mix it with the blue or you'll be
envious in every way,
What if you have a black heart and you are evil to the core,
Or red with a fiery angry rage, and you wish to
beat me to the floor,
What if you are simply beige and neither here nor there,
But if you're beige, I don't believe that you would even care,
Whatever colour you identify as in this world that
has gone quite mad,
I only ask that if you don't judge a person by their colour,
I'd be glad,
We are all one in this beautiful rainbow world that we all share,
And how wonderful it would be if for each other we would care,
So, I leave you with love in gold and caring in a purple hue,
Till hopefully one day we all we can all live in
a world of love anew

Sunset on my Journey

We build our empires of dirt and sand in our lives with such morbid pace,
Yet when we pass, they crumble and fall and leave behind barely a trace,
We worship things that don't exist, and show these things greatest respect,
While we brush aside those around us, as if they were nothing but a worthless insect,
We take rocks and oil from the ground, and value these more than life,
The news we watch each night yet remain unattached to the world in strife,
Have we lost the ability to love, to feel, and to care for those around us?
Am I the only one who feels the sorrow for this world we create with such furious fuss,
But this world I cannot change, the challenge too great, nor will I try to do so,
For I am content to change myself, and those that the way I will show,

*Love and an open heart will by my go to book that
I learn from and follow,*

*For the words of those gilded in robes and finery
I have found to be hollow,*

*Now as I near the end I have found my peace in
my own heart and soul,*

*And the two have come as one with my body,
and again has made me whole,*

*So do not try to change the world but merely change
in thyself and be true,*

*And the truth and the love that you learn,
will repair your broken pieces like glue.*

My Paradise

Have you ever been somewhere that was so quiet and serene,
Where the water was cool and crisp, and the air was fresh and clean,
When only the sound of wildlife filled the fresh clean air,
At night you would peruse the sky in total wonder as you stare,
A place where life's cares seemed to be so far away,
In the morning the sun would greet you with the warmth of a new day,
With a stream nearby for water and to wash away the grime,
You will feel totally connected to nature, whilst not having to watch the time,
The ocean, just half hours walk away, provides food including some big fish,
Which when cooked with forest herbs, provides a tasty dish,
Your city life now so far away it's just a memory now it seems,
Gladly would I trade city life to be here in my paradise, next to my cool crisp streams.

Harvest of Love

Time goes by and never stops to sleep,
But still rewards us with memories to keep,
Some bring happiness and some bring pain,
But in the end, they're lessons all the same,
They help us learn and help us grow,
We pass these lessons on as others we show,
How time can offer us the space to heal,
It gives us time to love and time to feel,
And though time is infinite, our lives here are not,
So please cherish the time here as we don't have a lot,

Words of Love and Understanding

When you read this, you will know I am talking to you,
Lay down your worries, your pain and your fears and rest in my heart,
You feel that no one understands, yet I understand you and your needs all too well,
You feel like you're alone, despite those around you,
You feel unloved, despite the words of those who tell you that they love you,
You feel worthless despite your true value,
Come and rest in my arms and in my heart.
Allow me to give you a hand and help you.
Not for reward but, merely out of love.
You are beautiful and worthwhile, though you do not see it.
So lay down your burdens and come and rest in my heart.

Conclusion

As we come to the end of this book of inspirational poetry, I hope that you have found words that have spoken to your heart, lifted your spirit, and given you hope as well as a reason to strive to go forward. Poetry has a unique way of stirring our emotions, surfacing deeper understandings, and inspiring us to reach within and then beyond ourselves.

Within the pages of this book, we have explored the rich tapestry of human feelings and experience including love, pain, resilience, courage, forgiveness, hope, and faith. May these poems fill you with strength when you are weak, comfort you in times of trouble, and guide you on your journey when you are lost.

Remember that you are never alone, and that even in the darkest of moments, there is always hope. The words I have written will hopefully continue to resonate with you long after you close this book and put it down, reminding you that your life has purpose and meaning, and that you are loved.

So, go out into the world and share your light with others, for you are part of the great tapestry that is humanity, and your own unique voice needs to be heard. Thank you for joining me on this poetic journey, and may it inspire you to write your own story of hope and transformation. Bless you all.

Acknowledgements

I would like to take this moment to express my heartfelt gratitude to all the people who have given me the inspiration and input that have helped shape me into the writer and poet that I am today. Your encouraging words and unwavering support have been my strength and motivation throughout this wonderful journey of writing a book of poetry.

Foremost, I would like to thank my parents, who instilled in me a love for literature and encouraged me to be creative from a young age. Their constant encouragement and support have been the pillars of my success, and it is because of them that I have found the courage to pursue my passion for writing.

I would also like to thank my friends and family for being my sounding boards, offering feedback, and for their kind words of praise during the ups and downs of my writing journey. Their unwavering support gave me the confidence to share my work with the world, and for that, I will always be grateful.

To my teachers, your passion for words ignited a love for poetry and writing within me that has only grown stronger over the years.

To Emily Gowor and her team for making this book possible. Her inspirational approach and the guidance she gave made my dream a reality.

Finally, I would like to thank my readers who have supported me by purchasing and reading my book. Your words of appreciation are what every writer dreams of, and I am humbled by your kind words.

To each and every one of you, I am forever grateful, and I hope that my book of poetry inspires others the way you have all inspired me.

About The Author

Ed is an author, and a man whose heart is filled with kindness, love, caring and compassion towards his fellow man. Ed is more than just a writer, he is a soulful individual who believes in the innate goodness of people and strives to not only bring out the best, but also look for the best in everyone.

His writing is a true reflection of his personal values and beliefs, and they are designed to inspire, motivate and heal readers to live a more fulfilling life and in turn for the reader to make a difference in someone else's life. Ed likens his writing to a balm for the soul, offering comfort and hope to those that are struggling or lost.

He is a beacon of light in a world that can sometimes be dark and unforgiving, and he is always trying to spread hope and positivity wherever he goes. If you are looking for an author who truly cares about people and wants to leave a legacy and make a genuine difference in the world, then Ed is the person you need to know.

Get to know Ed in his writings in this book and lookout for the next instalments of verse.

www.ingramcontent.com/pod-product-compliance
Lightning Source LLC
Chambersburg PA
CBHW051538010526
44107CB00064B/2768